THE SCIENCE DETECTIVE INVESTIGATES

Light

Katie Dicker

WAYLAND

First published in 2010 by Wayland

Copyright © Wayland 2010

Wayland
338 Euston Road
London NW1 3BH

Wayland Australia
Level 17/207 Kent Street
Sydney, NSW 2000

Produced for Wayland by
White-Thomson Publishing Ltd

www.wtpub.co.uk
+44 (0)845 362 8240

Senior editor: Camilla Lloyd
Designer: Clare Nicholas
Consultant: Jon Turney
Picture researcher: Amy Sparks
Illustrator: Stefan Chabluk
Sherlock Bones artwork: Richard Hook

British Library Cataloguing in Publication Data:
Dicker, Katie.
   Light. — (The science detective investigates)
   1. Light—Juvenile literature. 2. Light—Experiments—
   Juvenile literature.
   I. Title II. Series
   535-dc22

ISBN 978 0 7502 6020 6

Printed in China

Wayland is a division of Hachette Children's Books, an Hachette UK company.

www.hachette.co.uk

Picture Acknowledgments:
Abbreviations: t-top, b-bottom, l-left,
r-right, m-middle.
Cover: Dreamstime (Theo Gottwald)
Insides: Folios Dreamstime (Stuart
Key); **1** Dreamstime (Miklav); **4**
Shutterstock (Serg64); **5** NASA; **6**
Corbis (NASA/JPL-Caltech); **7** (t)
Dreamstime (Scol22), (b) Photolibrary
(Satoshi Kuribayashi); **8** Dreamstime
(Petar Zigich); **9** Dreamstime (Pryzmat);
10 Dreamstime (Paul Aniszewski);
11 Dreamstime (Miklav); **12** Getty
Images (Tariq Dajani); **13** Dreamstime
(Falcorpic), **14** Dreamstime (Jeffclow);
16 Dreamstime (Zigf); **17** (t)
Shutterstock (Victoria Visuals), (b)
Dreamstime (Dmitriy Shironosov);
18 Istockphoto (David Gunn); **19**
Dreamstime (Holgs); **21** Dreamstime
(l Chris Galbraith, r Indianeye); **22**
Photolibrary (John Rensten); **23**
Dreamstime (Jacek Chabraszewski);
24 Dreamstime (Godfer); **25**
Dreamstime (l Anette Romanenkol,
r Ali Ender Birer); **26** Dreamstime
(tr Theo Gottwald, bl Olena Abazid);
27 Dreamstime (Meedragon);
29 Corbis (Cydney Conger).

Contents

Words that appear in **bold** can be found in the glossary on page 30.

The Science Detective, Sherlock Bones, will help you learn all about Light. The answers to Sherlock's questions can be found on page 31.

What is light?

Light is a type of **energy**. It helps us to see everything around us. Light comes from different **sources**, such as the Sun or a light bulb. When the Sun rises each day, the sky brightens and we can see the world. If we turn on a light bulb in a dark room, objects become **visible** to us. Without light, our world would be in darkness.

Light and dark

During the day, most of our light comes from the Sun. The Sun gives out light and heat energy that people, plants and animals need to survive. At night, when the Sun goes down, there is no light and it is dark. In the day, it is also dark where sunlight cannot reach. It is dark inside caves and in the depths of the ocean, for example. At night or in dark places, we use other light sources, such as candles, torches or light bulbs to light up our world.

Why is it dark when you look under your bed or inside a cupboard?

▼ **The Sun is the main source of light on Earth.**

SCIENCE AT WORK

The Sun rises in the east and sets in the west. The Sun appears to move across the sky each day, but in fact the Sun stays still, while the Earth spins around. The Earth takes 24 hours to turn. At any time of day, one half of the planet is facing the sunlight, while the other half is in darkness.

▲ This photograph, taken close to the Moon, shows that one half of the Earth is in daylight, while the other half is in darkness.

THE SCIENCE DETECTIVE INVESTIGATES:

Seeing with light

You will need:
• shoe box with a lid • scissors • small everyday objects (such as pens, coins, paper clips, marbles) • sheet of A5 cardboard

1 Ask an adult to help you cut a small viewing hole at one end of the box, and a large hole (the size of a mug) in the box lid. Put some everyday objects into the box.
2 Cover the hole on the lid with the cardboard, so the inside of the box is in darkness. Look through the viewing hole. What can you see?
3 Move the cardboard 1 cm (0.5 in) at a time to let more light into the box. What can you see each time? Which objects are easiest to see? What colours can you see? Make a chart to record your findings.

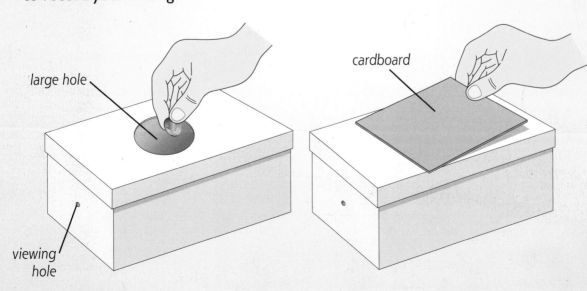

large hole

viewing hole

cardboard

What is natural light?

The Sun is the greatest source of natural light on Earth. This ball of burning hot gases is about 150 million kilometres (93 million miles) from our planet – it would take about 200 years to drive there! The Sun is so powerful that its heat and light energy reach us through space. Other sources of natural light include lightning and the glow of animals, such as fireflies.

Starlight

When something burns it gives out light as well as heat. We call this **incandescent light** (or hot light). The Sun is about 6,000°C (10,832°F) at its surface, and more than 15 million °C (27 million °F) at its centre. This heat warms our planet and fills our world with light. The Sun gives out a yellowy light. Smaller stars are dimmer and redder, while larger stars are brighter and bluer. Scientists look at the colours of distant stars using a **telescope**.

Lightning

Another type of incandescent light is lightning. During a thunderstorm, lightning causes a flash of light to streak across the sky. It gives out a very bright light, but only lasts for a fraction of a second. Lightning is a huge spark of **electricity** that forms in storm clouds, jumping from cloud to cloud or between clouds and the ground. Lightning can travel at 60 kilometres (37 miles) a second and is about five times hotter than the surface of the Sun.

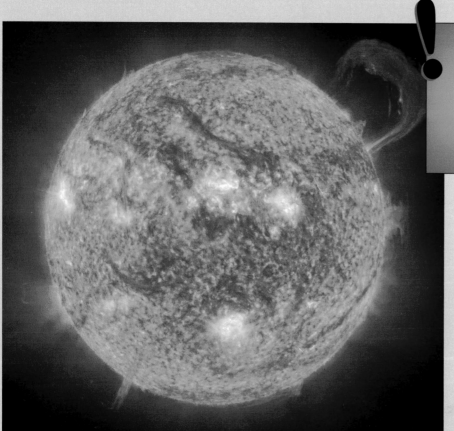

STAY SAFE

Never look at the Sun. It is dangerous because the Sun is too bright for your eyes and will harm your sight.

◄ **About one million Earths could fit inside the Sun – the closest star to our planet.**

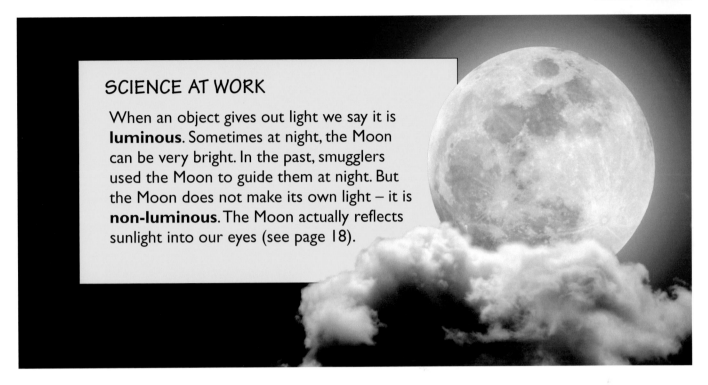

SCIENCE AT WORK

When an object gives out light we say it is **luminous**. Sometimes at night, the Moon can be very bright. In the past, smugglers used the Moon to guide them at night. But the Moon does not make its own light – it is **non-luminous**. The Moon actually reflects sunlight into our eyes (see page 18).

Cold light

Some objects give out light without heat. This is called **luminescent light** (or cold light). Luminescent light is produced by a chemical reaction. Fireflies and glow-worms, for example, make luminescent light using chemicals in their bodies. They use this light to attract a mate in the dark.

✿ Why do you think some deep-sea fish make their own light?

▼ When luminescent light comes from animals, such as glow-worms, it is called 'bioluminescence'.

What is artificial light?

Artificial light is light that we make ourselves. At night, or on a cloudy day, we use artificial light to help us see. We turn on a light bulb (powered by **mains electricity** or **batteries**) to brighten a room, we use car headlights to see the road ahead, and we use a candle to light up the dark.

Light bulbs

Traditional light bulbs have **filaments** that glow hot and give out light when electricity passes through them. We call them incandescent light bulbs. Newer, energy-saving light bulbs produce a type of luminescent light. These **fluorescent** light bulbs are filled with gas. When electricity passes through them, the gas causes a chemical on the inside of the glass to glow. **Neon lights** use gases, too. Some gases glow with a colour when electricity passes through them. They can also be used with coated glass to create different lighting effects. A light bulb gives out a bright or dim light depending on its size and type.

▼ **In a city, the artificial lights in offices mean that people can work when it is dark.**

Moving light

When light waves move away from
a light source, they spread out and
become less intense. The rays travel in
straight lines until they reach an object
that blocks their path. Light rays from
a strong light source, such as the Sun,
are bright and light up a large area.
Light rays from a weak light source,
such as a candle, are dim and light up
a smaller area.

🐾 **Why do you think light
travels faster in a vacuum?**

▶ **Light waves spread out
from a light bulb in straight
lines called beams or rays.**

▲ **The strong beam of light from a lighthouse
warns ships at sea of rocks or shallow water.**

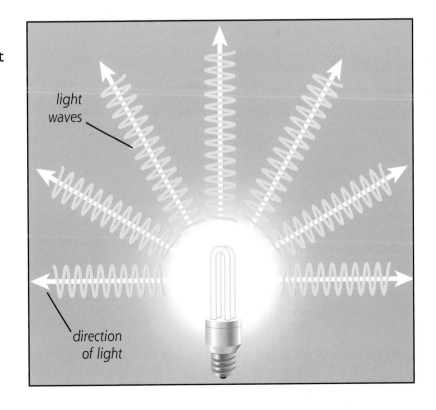

*light
waves*

*direction
of light*

Which materials let light through?

When light travels, it passes through some materials but cannot pass through others. We say that materials that let light through (such as glass) are **transparent**. Materials that let some light through (such as tracing paper) are **translucent**, and materials that let no light through (such as wood) are **opaque**.

Using materials

In our homes, we use some materials to let light in, and others to keep light out. Our windows are made from transparent glass to keep the rooms bright. Some windows are made with frosted glass or covered with net curtains. This makes the glass difficult to see through, but still lets some light through. In a bedroom, thick curtains help to keep out the light so the room is dark when you want to sleep.

Bright and dull

When the Sun shines in a clear sky, our surroundings are very bright. On a cloudy day, the world is less bright. It is still light, but the clouds have stopped some of the sunlight passing through. The clouds act like a translucent material.

▲ **Net curtains are used to cover a window, while allowing some light to pass through.**

🐾 **Why do you think we wear sunglasses?**

Lighting effects

Light bulbs are designed with transparent or translucent materials to create different lighting effects. Transparent light bulbs give out a bright light, while translucent light bulbs give out a dimmer, softer light. Lampshades can also affect the intensity of the light rays.

▶ **The size and shape of different light bulbs, and the type of glass used, creates different lighting effects.**

THE SCIENCE DETECTIVE INVESTIGATES:

Choosing materials

You will need:
• 5 shoe boxes, without lids • different materials (such as lace, white cotton, dark cotton, wool and denim), about 35 cm x 25 cm (14 in x 10 in) • sticky tape

1 Ask an adult to help you cut a small viewing hole at one end of each box.
2 Tape a piece of material tightly to the top of each box to make a lid.
3 Look through the viewing hole to compare the light and darkness in each box. Make a record of your findings. Which material would you choose to make bedroom curtains for a dark room? How would you ensure that your comparisons are fair?

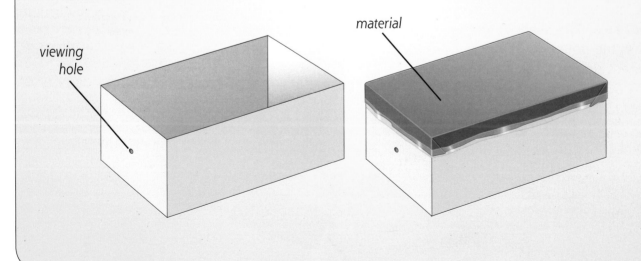

viewing hole

material

What are shadows?

Shadows are areas of darkness that form when an object stops light rays from passing through. The light rays cannot travel through the object or go around it, so a shadow forms. Opaque objects cause dark shadows. Translucent objects cause faint shadows because they let some light through.

Shadow shapes

A shadow is a similar shape to the object that causes it to form. When an object blocks light rays, the rays that pass its edges form the outline of the shadow. When a shadow forms in sunlight, it changes position and length depending on the time of day. At midday when the Sun is overhead, short shadows form on the ground because only a few light rays are blocked. In the morning and evening, the shadows are longer because the Sun's rays travel at an angle. This means that more light rays are blocked.

SCIENCE AT WORK

Sundials use shadows to tell the time. During the day, when the Sun moves across the sky, the position of a shadow changes. Sundials have a stick or pointer that forms a shadow on a marked 'clock face'. This shadow moves across the hourly markings at different times of day.

Earth rotates in a clockwise direction

sunlight

shadow

▲ When an object blocks sunlight, its shadow changes at different times of the day.

◀ When your body blocks rays of sunlight, a shadow forms the same shape on the ground.

Artificial light

We can create shadows with artificial light, too. When floodlights are used to light up a football stadium at night, you can see a shadow of the players on the pitch. When more than one floodlight is used, there are more shadows around each player. This is because the players block light rays from each floodlight as they move around the pitch.

🐾 **Why is your shadow shorter at midday than in the morning and evening?**

THE SCIENCE DETECTIVE INVESTIGATES:

Make a shadow puppet show

You will need:
• card • pencil • scissors • straws • sticky tape • table • lamp

1 Think of some characters for your show, such as people and animals, and draw them onto the card. Draw some props, too, such as trees and houses. Cut them out. Tape a straw to the back of each 'puppet' to hold it upright.
2 In a darkened room, put a lamp onto a table about 2 m (7 ft) away from a wall. Stand behind the table and hold your puppets in front of the light to create shadows on the wall.
3 Try moving your puppets towards the wall, and then towards the lamp. What do you notice? Why do you think this is? Can you make your small shadow puppets turn into huge monsters?

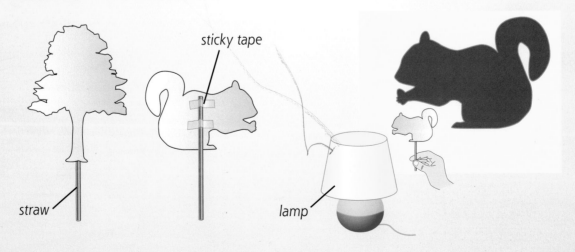

straw

sticky tape

lamp

What is reflection?

When light hits a surface, some of the light bounces off – rather like a ball bouncing off a hard surface. This is called **reflection**. When light is reflected, it changes direction. Different surfaces cause light rays to reflect in different ways.

Rough and smooth

When light rays hit a rough surface, some of the light is **absorbed** by the surface and the rays bounce off at different angles. This makes the surface appear dull. When light rays hit a smooth, flat surface, nearly all the light rays are reflected and they bounce off in the same direction. When you look in a smooth, shiny mirror, for example, nearly all the light reflects back into your eyes and you see a reflection of yourself.

▼ **Mirrors are made with a layer of smooth glass covering a layer of shiny metal. They reflect light into our eyes so we see a reflection.**

THE SCIENCE DETECTIVE INVESTIGATES:

Reflecting light

You will need:
• piece of thick A5 card • scissors • sheet of A4 white paper
• table • modelling clay • powerful torch • small mirror • pencil

1 Ask an adult to help you cut narrow slits in the sheet of card, to make a 'comb'.
2 Place the sheet of paper on a table in a darkened room. Stick the upright card comb to one end of the paper using modelling clay.
3 Lay the torch down to shine through the comb to separate the light rays. Hold the mirror at the other end of the paper.
4 Trace the path of the light rays with a pencil. What happens to the light when it hits the mirror? Now change the angle of the mirror. What happens this time?

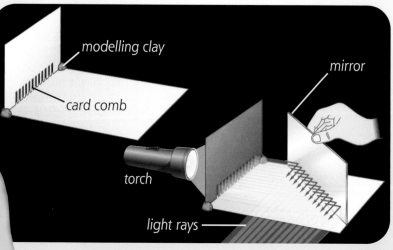

modelling clay

mirror

card comb

torch

light rays

SCIENCE AT WORK

Some animals have large eyes to help them to see in the dark. Tarsiers are found in Southeast Asia. These tiny creatures hunt at night. They have huge eyes in comparison to the size of their head. Their eyes – each as large as their brain – help the tarsier to spot other creatures in the darkness.

🐾 **Why do you think our pupils get bigger in dim light?**

THE SCIENCE DETECTIVE INVESTIGATES:

Make a pinhole camera

A pinhole camera works in a similar way to our eyes – it produces an upside down image. When we use our eyes, our brain turns the image around so we see it the right way up.

You will need:
• small square box without a lid (such as a gift box) • tracing paper • sticky tape • pin • lamp

1 Tape the tracing paper tightly over the open end of the box to make a screen.
2 Ask an adult to help you make a pinhole in the opposite side of the box.
3 In a darkened room, point the pinhole at the lamp. Look at the tracing paper screen. What do you notice?

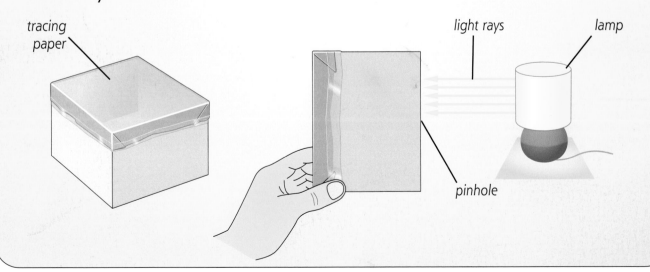

tracing paper

light rays

lamp

pinhole

What is refraction?

Light travels quickly through a vacuum or through gases such as air. But when light moves through transparent or translucent materials, it slows down. When light moves through glass, plastic or water, for example, the speed of light changes. When the light rays slow down, they also change direction. We call this **refraction**.

Changing direction

Light travels more slowly through transparent or translucent solids and liquids, than through air. This is because there are more **molecules** in solids and liquids to stop the light from moving. When light passes through a glass of water, for example, it slows down and changes direction as it moves from the air to the glass and water. As the light re-enters the air on the other side, it speeds up and changes direction again.

🐾 **If light bends through a transparent material, why do we see things clearly (without distortion) through a plain glass window?**

THE SCIENCE DETECTIVE INVESTIGATES:

Bending light rays

You will need:
• sheet of A5 card • square jar of water • powerful torch

1 Ask an adult to help you cut a narrow slit in the card.
2 In a darkened room, shine the torch through the slit and into the jar of water. What happens to the light rays?

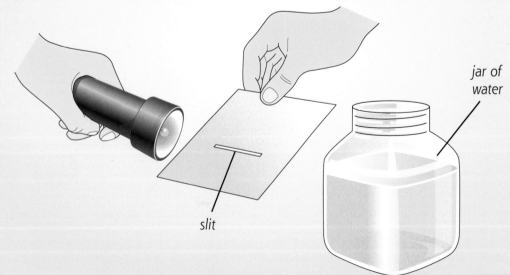

jar of water

slit

Refraction around us

If you place a drinking straw in a glass of water, it will appear to be bent or broken at the point where the straw meets the liquid. Have you ever tried to pick up an object in a swimming pool or a bowl of water and had difficulty touching what you see? These examples are caused by the refraction of light. Light rays from the straw, or the object in water, change direction when they move from the water to the air and reach your eyes. This makes it look like they have moved from their real position.

▶ **The stem of this flower appears to be broken because the light rays have refracted.**

▼ **Eagles learn to judge distances carefully, to take account of refraction when they catch fish from the water.**

What are lenses?

A lens is a piece of curved transparent material, such as glass or plastic. When light passes through a lens, it refracts and changes direction. Lenses are curved inwards or outwards to change the path of a light ray. We use lenses to make objects look bigger, smaller or nearer.

Convex lenses

Convex lenses are wider in the middle than at the edges. They cause light rays to bend inwards and make objects look bigger. A magnifying glass is a convex lens. It can be used to examine small objects. Our eyes have a convex lens that helps to focus light rays at the back of our eye.

Concave lenses

Concave lenses are thinner in the middle than at the edges. They cause light rays to bend outwards and make objects look smaller and clearer. A viewing hole in a door uses a concave lens to see people on the other side. The lens makes a person look much smaller than they really are.

▲ The concave lens in this viewing hole makes it possible to see who has come to the door.

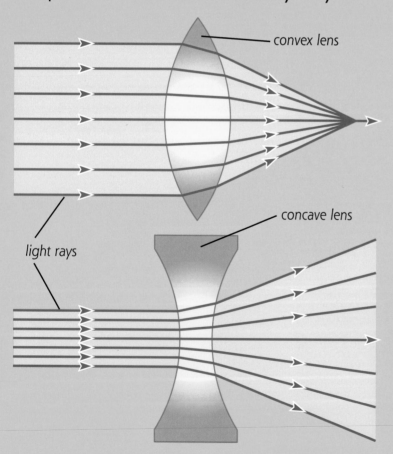

convex lens

concave lens

light rays

◄ Convex lenses refract light rays inwards to make objects look bigger. Concave lenses refract light rays outwards to make objects look smaller.

THE SCIENCE DETECTIVE INVESTIGATES:

Make a magnifying glass

You will need:
• round-bottomed flask (or spherical bowl, such as a fish bowl) • water
• newspaper or magazine

1 Fill the flask (or bowl) with water to make a curved lens.

spherical bowl of water

newspaper

2 Look through the side of the bowl and hold a newspaper or magazine close to the other side. What do you notice about the text on the page? What happens when you move the paper closer or further away?

🐾 **What type of lens does a magnifying glass have? What is it used for?**

SCIENCE AT WORK

Magnifying glasses have been known to start fires. The convex lens in a magnifying glass causes light rays to bend inwards. If the Sun's rays are refracted towards a single point, the area can become very hot and may start to burn.

▼ **This girl's eye looks bigger through a magnifying glass.**

How do we use lenses?

Lenses are very useful in our lives. We use them to look more closely at the things around us. Lenses can be used to correct bad eyesight. They are also used in instruments such as **microscopes** and telescopes that help us to see objects that would otherwise be invisible to us.

Spectacles

Spectacles are made with convex or concave lenses. They help to focus images on the back of our eyes so we see things clearly. **Short-sighted** people find it difficult to see things in the distance. Their eyes cause light rays to focus in front of the retina, which makes the image appear 'out of focus'. Concave lenses bend the light rays outwards to focus on the retina and sharpen the image. **Long-sighted** people find it difficult to see things close-up because their eyes cause light rays to focus 'behind' the retina. Convex lenses bend the light rays inwards to focus on the retina and make the image clearer.

🐾 **Bifocal lenses are good for people who are both short-sighted and long-sighted. What type of lens are they? Use the Internet to help you.**

▼ **This girl is long-sighted. She uses glasses with convex lenses to make the text of her book look sharper and clearer.**

Magnifying instruments

Binoculars, telescopes and microscopes are instruments that use convex lenses. Binoculars and telescopes make far away objects look much nearer. Like powerful magnifying glasses, these lenses cause light rays to bend inwards to enlarge an image. Microscopes use a series of convex lenses to make tiny objects look hundreds or thousands of times bigger than they really are.

leaf veins

SCIENCE AT WORK

In the 1800s, lace makers used spherical glass bottles of water as a type of lens. The bottles focused candlelight onto small areas of their work so they could see the fine details more clearly.

◀▼ **A microscope helps you to see these leaf veins in more detail.**

How do we see colours?

Everything we see around us has a colour. We see these colours when light reflects into our eyes. Sunlight looks white but it is actually a mixture of coloured light. We call these colours the '**light spectrum**'.

Different wavelengths

The light waves in sunlight have wavelengths of different colours – red, orange, yellow, green, blue, indigo and violet light. When these colours combine, they make 'white light'. You can see the light spectrum when light shines through a glass prism. Each wavelength slows down and is refracted by a different amount – violet light slows and bends the most, while red light slows and bends the least. This causes the colours to separate out and form a 'rainbow'.

▶ **When light shines through a prism, the colours of light refract in different ways to form a rainbow.**

◀ **Raindrops act like tiny prisms when sunlight passes through them. This forms a rainbow in the sky.**

Seeing colour

Our eyes see red, green and blue light, or a combination of these colours. We see colours when objects reflect or absorb the colours in white light. When objects absorb some of the wavelengths, only a few colours are reflected into our eyes. If red and green light is reflected, for example, we see yellow. If all the colours are reflected, we see white light.

▼ Red, green and blue light combine to make different colours and shades.

🐾 What colours do you think combine to make turquoise, purple and white light?

Your project: Light in action

The way light travels and is reflected changes what we see in our world. Try this activity to explore the movement of light, the behaviour of lenses and the colours that light contains.

You will need:
- round-bottomed flask (or spherical bowl, such as a fish bowl) • water • newspaper
- tealight candle • sheet of white card
- small mirror • modelling clay • torch

Method

1 Fill the flask with water and place the lit candle more than 30 cm (12 in) from the bowl. In a darkened room, hold the card against the other side of the bowl. Move it away until you see an image of the candle flame on the card. What do you notice about the image?

2 Lift the candle up slightly. What happens to the image? Now move the candle closer to the bowl. What happens this time?

3 Look through the bowl at the candle on the other side. What do you notice about the candle? Now blow out the candle.

4 Put a small mirror in the water. Use the modelling clay to place it at an angle. Shine a torch onto the mirror. Hold the sheet of card in front of the mirror until a rainbow appears (you may need to change the angle of the torch, the angle of the mirror or the position of the card to see your rainbow). Why does a rainbow appear?

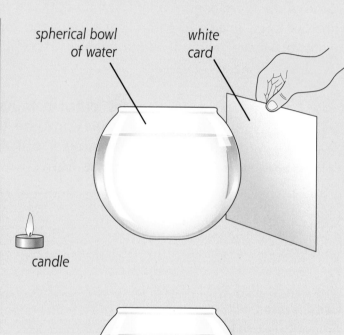

spherical bowl of water

white card

candle

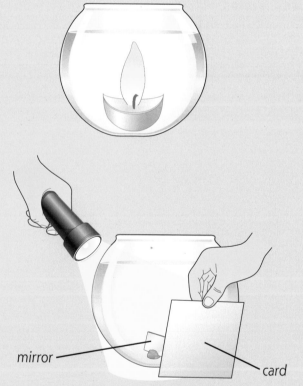

mirror

card

What happened and why?

The image of the candle flame on the card is upside down. This is because the light rays have refracted as they pass through the bowl of water, and have crossed over. When the candle moves up, the image moves down. When the candle moves closer to the bowl, the image moves further away and eventually disappears from the card. When you look at the candle through the bowl, the candle looks bigger because the bowl of water acts like a magnifying lens. A rainbow appears on the card because the bowl of water acts like a prism, refracting the torchlight. The mirror reflects the light so it passes back through the bowl and refracts even more. This splits the white light into different colours.

▼ **A fish bowl acts like a lens and bends the light rays that pass through it. The only light rays that don't bend are the ones that pass through the centre of the bowl.**

Glossary

absorbed When something is retained, instead of being reflected or transmitted. Light rays are absorbed when they hit dull surfaces.

battery A portable device that contains chemicals that react to produce electricity.

concave mirror A mirror that curves inwards. Concave mirrors reflect light rays outwards and make objects look bigger.

convex mirror A mirror that curves outwards. Convex mirrors reflect light rays inwards and make objects look smaller.

electricity A type of energy. Lightning is a type of static electricity that jumps from one material to another. Mains electricity is a type of electricity that flows. We use it to power artificial lights and machines.

energy The ability to do work. Light energy helps us to see. Heat energy warms things up.

filament The thin wire in an incandescent light bulb, which heats up and gives out light when electricity passes through it.

fluorescent A type of luminescent light that glows.

focus The point at which light rays come together. Light rays focus on the back of the eye, for example.

fuel A material that is used to provide energy.

incandescent light The light that is given out by a hot object.

iris The part of the eye that makes the pupil bigger or smaller to let more or less light through.

lens A curved transparent material, such as glass, that causes light rays to change direction.

light spectrum All the different colours that make up light rays. The light spectrum also includes colours we cannot see.

long-sighted When someone can see things clearly in the distance, but not close-up.

luminescent light The light produced by a chemical reaction that does not involve burning or heating.

luminous An object that gives out light, such as a torch or a candle.

mains electricity Electricity that is supplied to homes, offices and schools through a grid system.

materials What things are made of. Wood, stone and wool are all materials.

microscope An instrument that uses lenses to make objects look hundreds or thousands of times bigger than they really are.

molecules Tiny particles that make up a substance. Molecules are made of two or more atoms.

neon light A luminescent light that uses a chemical reaction with neon gas to produce light.

non-luminous An object that does not give out light. A book is a non-luminous object, for example.

opaque A material that does not let light pass through it. You cannot see through opaque materials.

pupil The hole at the front of the eye, that lets light into the eye.

reflection When something bounces off a surface. Light rays are reflected from a mirror, for example.

refraction The slight bend in light rays when they pass between air and another transparent material.

short-sighted When someone can see things clearly close-up, but not in the distance.

source The origin of something.

telescope A device that uses lenses to magnify distant objects.

translucent A material that only lets some light pass through it. You cannot see clearly through translucent materials.

transparent A material that lets light pass through it. You can see clearly through transparent materials, such as glass.

vacuum An empty space that contains no air.

visible When an object can be clearly seen.

wave A movement up and down. Light rays travel in waves.

wavelength The distance from the crest of one wave to the crest of the next wave. Light rays are made up of colours that have different wavelengths.

Answers

Page 4: It is dark under your bed or inside a cupboard because light cannot reach there.

Page 5: At first, the shoe box will be quite dark. As you move the card and let more light in, you should find that objects that are light in colour are easier to see than objects that are dark in colour. Shiny objects, such as coins, will also be more visible because any light that enters the box will reflect from them into your eyes.

Page 7: Deep-sea fish make their own luminescent light because they live in the dark parts of the ocean. They use this light to find their way in the dark, to attract a mate (or prey to eat), or to protect themselves from other creatures.

Page 9: Example answers: ceiling light, lamp, torch, car headlights or brake lights, emergency vehicle light, computer light, warning/indicator lights (for a cooker, heater or printer, for example), neon sign, digital clock, spotlight, floodlight, bonfire, fireworks, candle, glow stick.

Page 11: Light travels faster in a vacuum because there are no materials to stop the light from moving.

Page 12: We wear sunglasses to protect our eyes from bright sunlight. Sunglasses are made from a translucent material that only lets some light through.

Page 13: You would choose the material that blocked most light to make bedroom curtains for a dark room. To make your comparisons fair, you would need to use the same sized viewing hole in each box. The material would also need to be taped tightly, so no additional light shines through at the sides.

Page 15: Your shadow is shorter at midday because when the Sun is overhead, your body blocks fewer light rays. In the morning or evening, the Sun's rays reach your body at an angle so more of your body blocks more light rays.

Page 15: The shadow puppet grows larger if you move it towards the lamp and smaller if you move it towards the wall. The closer the puppet is to the lamp, the more light waves are blocked. This creates a bigger shadow.

Page 16: The light rays travel in straight lines towards the mirror and bounce off the mirror. If you change the angle of the mirror, the reflections change direction. The light rays are reflected at the same angle as they hit the mirror.

Page 17: Sunlight sparkles on the surface of the sea because sunlight reflects from the smooth surface of the water. The ripples cause the light to bounce off the smooth surface in different directions.

Page 19: Our pupils get bigger in dim light to let more light into our eyes so we can see images clearly.

Page 19: You should see an upside down reflected image of the lamp on the screen because the light rays have crossed over.

Page 20: Refraction occurs when light passes through a window, but the effect is cancelled out. Light rays are bent in one direction when they hit the window, but they bend in the other direction when they pass to the air on the other side.

Page 20: The light rays bend as they enter the jar (when they pass from air to glass/water) and bend back again as they leave the jar (when they pass from glass/water to air).

Page 23: The bowl of water acts like a convex lens and makes the newspaper or magazine print bigger. When you move the paper closer to the bowl, the size of the type gets smaller. When you move the paper further away from the bowl, the type gets bigger.

Page 23: A magnifying glass has a convex lens. It is used to make objects look bigger.

Page 24: Bifocal lenses are used in some spectacles. They are a combination of convex and concave lenses. A concave lens in the top part of the bifocal lens helps with distance vision. A convex lens in the bottom part of the bifocal lens helps with close vision. They are useful for people who are long- and short-sighted.

Page 27: We see a combination of coloured light in the following ways: blue and green light combine to make turquoise light; blue and red light combine to make purple light; blue, green and red light combine to make white light.

Websites

http://science.howstuffworks.com/light.htm
Find out more about light and how it works.

http://www.physics4kids.com/files/light_intro.html
Learn more about light, colours and lenses.

http://www.exploratorium.edu/snacks/iconlight.html
Try some experiments to investigate light and colour.

http://www.bbc.co.uk/schools/ks2bitesize/science/activities/see_things.shtml
Some fun online activities about reflecting mirrors.

http://www.learner.org/teacherslab/science/light
Try some activities about colours and the laws of light.

http://library.thinkquest.org/27356/index.htm
Read more about natural and artificial light and find out how light is used in technology.

http://www.colormatters.com
Learn more about sight and how we use colours.

http://www.sciencenewsforkids.org
Keep up with the latest news about light and its uses.

Index

The Science Detective Investigates

Contents of titles in the series:

Electricity
978 0 7502 6017 6

What is electricity?
Where does electricity come from?
Why do we need batteries?
How does electricity flow?
When does the flow of electricity stop?
Why do we use circuits?
What are conductors?
What are insulators?
What are switches?
How can you change a circuit?
Why do we use electrical symbols?
Is our use of electricity harming the environment?
Your project: How does the length of wire change a bulb's brightness?

Forces and Motion
978 0 7502 6022 0

What are forces?
What are balanced forces?
How do forces change an object's shape?
How do forces change the way things move?
What is gravity?
What is friction?
What is air resistance?
What is water resistance?
Why do objects float and sink?
What is pressure?
How do we use forces?
What are levers and pulleys?
Your project: Investigating forces

Light
978 0 7502 6020 6

What is light?
What are natural sources of light?
What is artificial light?
How does light travel?
Which materials let light through?
What are shadows?
What is reflection?
How do we use light to see?
What is refraction?
What are lenses?
How do we use lenses?
How do we see colours?
Your project: Light in action

Magnets and Springs
978 0 7502 6019 0

What is magnetism?
Which materials are magnetic?
What is a magnetic field?
Is the Earth a magnet?
Are all magnets the same?
How do we use magnets?
How is magnetism used by trains?
What is a spring?
What happens when you stretch or compress a spring?
Why are spring loaded objects useful?
How are springs used in measuring?
How are springs used in suspension?
Your project: How can you make a compass?

Sound
978 0 7502 6021 3

What is sound?
How does sound travel?
How do humans hear?
How do other animals hear?
Are all sounds the same?
How do we make sounds with our voices?
What is music?
What is sound insulation?
What is an echo?
How is sound used?
How do we measure sound?
Are there sounds that humans cannot hear?
Your project: Which state of matter does sound travel through best?

Materials
978 0 7502 6018 3

What are materials?
How do we use materials?
What are solids and liquids?
What are gases?
What is evaporation?
What is condensation?
When do materials melt and freeze?
How does heat change materials?
What are mixtures and solutions?
Which materials can be squashed and stretched?
What are conductors and insulators?
What will materials be like in the future?
Your project: Testing materials

WAYLAND